GW01046077

The Method Men

DAVID BRIGGS was born in 1972, and grew up in the New Forest. He lives in Bristol, where he is Head of English at the Grammar School. He received an Eric Gregory Award in 2002. *The Method Men* is his first collection.

The Method Men

David Briggs

London

PUBLISHED BY SALT PUBLISHING
Fourth Floor, 2 Tavistock Place, Bloomsbury, London WC1H 9RA United Kingdom

Salt Publishing 2010

Printed in Great Britain by the MPG Books Group, Bodmin and King's Lynn

Typeset in Swift 9.5 / 13

ISBN 978 1 84471 728 6 hardback

1 3 5 7 9 8 6 4 2

for Jane Wolf

Contents

Acknowledgements

Grateful acknowledgements are due to the editors of the following publications in which some of these poems, or versions of them, first appeared: *Agenda Broadsheets*, *The Frogmore Papers*, *The Guardian*, *Horizon Review*, *Iota*, *Limelight*, *Magma*, *Notes from the Underground*, *NthPosition*, *Poetry Life*, *Poetry Review* and *Poetry Wales*. 'My Year of Culture' gained a commendation in the 2007 National Poetry Competition. 'Eleven Ante-Meridian' was broadcast on BBC Radio Bristol in 2003.

An early version of 'David Briggs *Landscape and Liability*' appeared, as the title suggests [sic], to musical accompaniment on my first album *Landscape and Liability* (Unreal Records, 1999). Some of these poems appeared first in the anthology *Reactions* 5, Ed. Clare Pollard (Pen & Inc Press, 2005). Others are due to appear in the anthology *Identity Parade*, Ed. Roddy Lumsden (Bloodaxe, 2010).

I am grateful to the Society of Authors for an Eric Gregory Award in 2002. I should also like to thank Matthew Caley, Gareth Jones, David Selwyn and, most of all, Roddy Lumsden for their advice on many of these poems, and for help in assembling the collection.

The Method Men

'. . . a style
Our lives bring with them: habit for a while,
Suddenly they harden into all we've got . . .'

— PHILIP LARKIN 'Dockery and Son'

Twenty Below Zero

After reaching the peninsula
we received a silver bullet,
edges flecked with powder, as a gift.

Steam from Turkish coffee
syrupped through our window
in the marbled night.

Wrapped in bear pelts we huddled
on the stone floor, turning it over
in our hands, memorising duels

we had fought on our way to the sea.

Woodland, with Two Figures

As roe deer dip like ploughs
through the forest floor's furrows,
they lie surveying each other,
without binoculars,
and he is permitted to span
the ha-ha of her estate
with the cunning of poachers.

These will be snared moments, at best.
Then, in the way feminine intuition
came to be judged witchcraft,
he may recoil
like a discharged hunting-rifle,
trace faint smoke-trails hearthwards
through leaves dry as scripture.

Yet, something will ignite between them:
a bonfire of inhibitions,
from which the fresh-raked debris
of this profligate season
may take flight—cinders on thermal draughts
into spiralling winds
seeking remembered origins.

Like Roma around a campfire
they begin to imagine
new Englands of the heart—
what might have been had they found
each other sooner. Without speech,
or signature, they form a small
republic of love, which will endure.

Historia Occultica

Scrying evolved during the early
Cuckoo period: an old crone,
exiled to the thick of the wood,

saw through her crude glass darkly,
for a fee. One might pay with duck eggs,
robed in night to avoid arcane

imputations of devilry. And
we are led to wonder just
what, exactly, she could see:

damsel-tupping goatswains?
measure-cheating merchants?
the clause in a ripening Will?

All grist to her mill, as she
sat picking through the offal
of lone wealth and longevity.

The Method Men

Carson found the pregnant heifer
by releasing his canniest cockerel

dead centre in its coop and staggering
the same pattern of steps across pasture.

He might confirm a rough, east-by-south-east route
from patterns in loosely-scattered grain.

If he then clubbed the newborn to death
after studying its amniotic membrane,

and opened its bloody entrails
on the nearest boulder like a book,

it was said he read nature fluently.
But Woodward saw cuckold horns in his own hearth

on Lammas Eve. So, he pitched a lamb's
shoulder bone on the flames and wept gladly

at the confirmation of its cracking.
A westward flutter of swifts helped Metcalfe

learn the name of the man who had stolen
his butter quern. And McIvor always

pitched his tent where a chain-swung amulet
suggested a bed of soft sediment.

Both men made their bread discerning
the lines etched by Fate in palms and foreheads.

Me, I always learned enough by firing
my full quiver of arrows at random

and observing the manner of their falling.
Or, when that failed, I could always find

omens in your first words each morning.

Rural Push, Urban Push

The River tightens its belt and, bloated
with alluvium, bulges over each bank.
How then, should he dare to cross?

Slaked with sewage, scuffed boots squelch
about the jetty. He is one-hundred-
and-one years late for the last ferry.

Having walked too far today already,
he rummages in sackcloth trouser pockets
for clay pipe and tinderbox.

As marigold smoke skeins out across water,
a vision of Norman horsemen
fords the River towards him:

equine necks straining through currents;
scabbards crudely slapping on flanks;
chain mail rippling hypnotically forward . . .

He waves his letter of introduction
by way of surrender. The River
waves back as he returns to the road.

Closed Systems

The night wears stars; he wears his shirt
unbuttoned. Badgers amble across floodplains

towards him. Now, a thin *tranche* of moon,
partial and blotted: a strange time

for divining. He is transplanting water—
stream to river to estuary—

in a teacup and an unbroken line
from the east to the west coast; but,

stooping to the river he sometimes stops,
cognisant, perhaps, of madness in his method,

or his father's ghost swimming the cold water.
When thunder rends the sky he recalls

the rising water table of his childhood;
raindrops collecting in teacups placed

for that purpose on the back doorstep;
always something upsetting his fieldwork.

Drought

Dirt-storm dust, light as conscience,
puffed up by wind gusts,
by footfalls, by combines—

ghost of Earth; Id of alluvium.
Fast in the knap of a best suede jacket,
billowing from backslaps:

ingratiating itself;
lingering in crevices;
insisting on an appointment.

Dust nourishing nothing;
swarming lightly through Summer,
its porch steps and orange groves;

expanding its Empire of Nil
among wheatrows, in gutters, in pithcraters.
Rain is either hearsay or heresy.

What to Burn When You've Burnt Your Bridges

Ten years he claimed he'd been travelling.
The beard fell authentically on his chest
like a medal. He wasn't extending
a metaphor, in the way some might claim
any manner of existence as a form
of 'travelling' when viewed in the right light.

Ten years on the road, of no fixed abode;
genuine wanderlust through civil wars,
deserts, plains, colonies and kasbahs.
Crow's feet perched with a predatory gait
on his milk-sick eyes, while we guessed his age.
'So, has it changed you much?' the Dutch girl asks.
He claps open calloused palms, conjuring
an old, passport-sized photograph of himself.

Better to ask what it was that drove
him to exile when only a boy:
eyes wide as moons about to break
orbit from a faithless planet; the smile
fixed as an African border; but, this
is a question he doesn't seem disposed
to answer. I choose not to ask.

Better to pass him the kif; call for more
coffee and hookah; watch his match burn blue,
then green, as it laps up the celluloid;
reach across the backgammon board to catch
the ashes, even if there is no wind
this wakeful night in which to scatter them.

The Dispossessed Lion Tamer, with Sprung Padlock

A sprung padlock rattles in the hinged hasp
of a wind-flung, gridiron, cage door.
The oak-board floor swept clean of bedding straw,
and the dispossessed lion tamer gasps
at threats in the cut-and-paste newsprint
ransom note. Such is the way of disaster:
ruin falls always from an unforeseen quarter.

One might have imagined a different
end to his career. He can't raise the cash.
The in-tent circus counsellor suggests
clowning, till he can meet the note's request.
He tries whiskey; kills time with the lash
of a drunken whip, roaring at the crime:
A man without his lion is merely marking time.

What Happened to Clowns

i.m. Miroslav Holub

when nobody laughed any more?
When even the act of pouring
hot custard down Pantalone's
hoop-waisted trews
failed to simmer even a snigger?
Clowns took to the streets.
Hyperbolic, red and yellow boots
flip-flopped uptown; the afternoon so hot,
buckets of confetti couldn't cool them off.
And they congregated at the railings
of the offices of the Minister for Circus.
Years of inadequate investment
had whittled their craft to politics
they didn't have the heart for.
Perhaps, they ought to have become
taxi drivers? Writing had been on walls—
or had been, before Scaramouche blacked
the writing over with arches of paint
to connote railway tunnels,
against which they had squandered
engine-red and canary-yellow striped,
plywood locomotives.
While they disputed for spokespersons
through mime, Pierrot posed forlornly
at the Doric-framed doorstep
of the offices of the Minister for Circus,
only to pirouette abjectly back
to mutinous crowds when the bell-push
streamed water that smudged his mascara,
tickled the wrinkles of his face.
Tweedledee and Tweedledum took
to beating each other's craniums
with styrofoam crowbars, blundering

about pavements in elaborate plays
of faux semi-consciousness.
No one so much as smiled.
It was merely tragic—two ageing clowns
resorting to clichéd slapstick.
Even those veterans who claimed
to have trained with Aristophenes
failed to find euphemisms
by which to allude to the shifting paradigm
of their times. In the distance,
four pantomime horsemen came
careering and whinnying toward them.

Père Lachaise

Burn Your Own Demons!

—JAMES DOUGLAS MORRISON
Translation of the inscription on his tomb

Not ravens, as we'd been expecting,
on his granite headstone, but scented
envelopes and *Chivas Regal* bottles,
CND buttons and gladioli,

Lucky Strike packets, votive candles,
silk panties, fingernails, peyote bark,
witch hazel, conical reefers,
photographs, vials, snakeskins, hair,

handwritten sonnets.
From behind the sepulchre, another pilgrim.
Veritable pilgrim. He squats square on
to the bronze, legend-bearing plaque:

KAWA TON DAIMONA EAYTOY;
magics a bottle of *Martell* from his coat
and sucks like a gunnery officer;
wraps brown resin in *Rizla*;

lights the fanned touchpaper of his slight
torpedo with a flick of the gunflint
in his *Zippo* lighter. He slams the lid
shut like a starboard hatch against brine,

leaving a faint whiff of paraffin.
He submits to its unguent accuracy.
He is stardust. He is golden.
He digs this cemetery. It's, like, a garden.

The Ghosts of Highgate Cemetery

in frowsy, mutton-sleeved grave-clothes,
clockless, cold and sepia
in the bucolic lanes between tombs,

come visiting two-and-two,
bearing guineas and barley cakes,
and they draw together as curtains

at graves of the newly interred.
There are courteous introductions;
calling cards are left to lean hopefully

at the more baroque mausoleums.
You think you might settle into this,
as a toast is raised to cool draughts

from the Fleet, lesser-known river
of the Underworld, whose waters confer
anonymity, distinction or infamy

according to inscrutable principles.

On the Banks of Acheron

What is the sound of waiting for Charon?
It's the silence of granite,
the nothing of worm casks,
alluvial whispers,
tinnitus whistle,
hearing aid feedback;
your cochlea struck like timpani
by a regrettable memory;
your mind's song played backwards
through industrial speakers;
demented scratching
of cocaine-fuelled cardiographs
across all of which, first distant,
then sure, the plash of his bone oar
sweeping through water.

What did you see from that shore?
I saw waters like coal tar
dank on the bedding grit,
boiling alembics of river-rock alchemy;
mists shaped like stillborns,
like gibbets,
like scorpions.

Did you smell him first? Yes.
Was it musk-fox or wolf-breath? Neither.
Is he death-cold or fever-hot? Both.

With what did you pay him?
With everything.

Asking the Difficult Questions

just as he might break into the deserted house,
sidle crabwise the sag-sad doorframe,
retract a steadying hand from its splintered lintel;

as he might scuff up dust and dead spiders,
the browned, thinly strewn newsprint;
bat the bare bulb, set it swinging like Tyburn;

he might pause in the silence, count the Deathwatch
tick-tock from doomed joists and rafters;
might risk gingerly the febrile staircase,

tread the pepper-shot landing, shoulder a door,
jemmy the wardrobe, set coat hangers jangling,
run a finger through dust on the dresser;

collapse on mouldering bedclothes, sigh
from his stomach, sleep through the sirens—far off,
somewhere other; and hunker there gladly: his head

a deserted house, into which no one has broken.

Attic Clearance

At first, I'm faithful to the whole shebang:
a tinplate humming top I wound and span

in Grandma's front room, rapt in appalled study
of her arthritic hands rattling the tea tray;

a model farmyard I glued together
one wet morning, while Mother scratched through

bank statements, pecked into her purse.
We were broken eggshell when Father chose

another coop to play cock-a-doodle.
Thirty years since I looked up 'divorce'

in this *Heinemann School Dictionary*,
and began to fill these forgotten notebooks

with some of the other big words.
So much stuff hoarded. I don't know why.

It's a compilation album of the B-sides of life;
or, here's how it should be understood:

a time capsule marked for my adult self
that's better left buried in childhood.

High Summer, 1979

I'm not conscious of Margaret Thatcher,
and Father is still immortal—
for another year or so.

I spend my days camouflaging
the corrugated tin roof of my bunker
with soil and windfalls and foliage,

armed with a washing-up liquid bottle,
vacuum-filled with water from the pond.
Soon, they will find me,

and then we will watch *Quatermass.*
I'll wake from the same nightmare
of nuclear apocalypse,

and decide it's preferable
to be blown to bits,
even if Stuart thinks his brown belt

in Judo will see *our* gang safely
through the inevitable phase
of post-fallout anarchy.

I considered well how best to spend
my four, post-warning minutes.
The ambition in those lists!

All those things I've yet to tick off.

Testicular Torsion

A phrase that entered my vocabulary
as a bolt hurled by a sadistic god,
or a drunk driver
headaching through a playground
on bald tyres.
To learn it was common,
might come to diagnose any of us—
not just James ________ of 5A,
the void of whose absence
had been explained by the School's
many doctors *manqué*—
was a hard truth to discover:
a difficult phrase to say.
But we all practised alone
à la Demosthenes—
one rock-hard word in each cheek.

High Summer, 1989

We dandied along the primrose path,
through the heyday of Stock-Aitken-Waterman,
in our purple velvet jackets

and ox-blood *Doc Martens*;
Marlboros vased in the saggy back pockets
of faded blue *Levis*.

We'd take the short cut through
the Hill Lane cemetery gates,
microanalyse *The Queen is Dead*,

compose execrable lyrics
for songs in the key of drone.
The tortured types. A walking groan.

Scornful of the unholy marriage
between a straight life
and hidden fetish—

the vicar in his tutu—
and cast adrift in a philistine world,
we walked in beauty, like clichés.

'They Miss Him Most Who Loved Him Best'

For Leonard Herbert Briggs

Steeped in sunlight,
this slab of black marble
pinning Earth's crust to its mantle—

a canvas sheet that might flap free
in high wind—becomes a portal
to Death's espaliered orchard.

So gently struck, the chapel bell
ordains these rare hours sacred.
Mossed turf. Feet that hitch-hiked

on the steel toes of your Police-issues,
skipped two strides to your one,
turn away from your repose—

only my own height's distance below.

The inscription on my father's headstone; commissioned by his second wife and her children.

Required Reading

I know it's something to do with multiples of four,
but I'm moved to interpret the six blank pages
that conclude Miroslav Holub's final collection,

The Rampage, as a ludic last 'word' of challenge
for the reader; although, they might equally well
represent a few bars of awed, pre-applause silence;

or, given the hard following on by death
from publication, the invisible score
of a proleptic, John Cage-y Requiem.

I guess it's a matter of presses and bindings,
but I find lines flitting across these blank leaves,
as though cast by eidetic zoetrope—and,

in this echoey vault, into which I have stepped
unwittingly, aware that many books
do not deserve their blanks, that this one does

(and that I do not understand them),
I turn back to the beginning and face
'The Wall in the Corner by the Stairs'.

A Portrait of the English Technician

Now, at last, central government is telling them not just what to teach, but how to teach it. The process of turning teachers into technicians continues.

— PAUL TROWLER *Education Policy*

The English Technician will wear carmine jackets,
and one shoe marked 'High',
and one shoe marked 'Low'.
The English Technician will abandon the photocopying
to Arctic winds lurching through the schoolyard
like overdeveloped schoolboys, because
he has sensed something divine
in that bell-bordered wasteland.
He will brew the perfect pot of peppermint tea;
recite Soyinka while spooning the sugar;
remark that the quality of the evening sky
is like a delicate filigree of Transvaal silver
he received from a blind, Egyptian carpet merchant
in exchange for a *contretemps* about Chatterton.
The English Technician will ride
a green, butcher's bicycle through the school gates
one minute before the bell every morning.
The English Technician will often be unnecessary,
but always elegant.
He will sometimes be found
rubbing earth into his cheeks
because he has forgotten the battles
of Sherra-moor and Agincourt.
He will sometimes be found rubbing earth
into other people's cheeks.
In winter people will cry,
'Where is the English Technician?'
because they believe the sky to be falling.
It will be difficult to know clearly

what the English Technician is thinking,
as he brings you books opened to pages
you had not formerly known to exist.

The Library of Missed Ripostes

Where everyone has their own desk lamp,
and meticulously indexed shelves loom,

like anecdotes collected for some long overdue
work of biographical back-stabbery.

No one behind the desk, just now.
But for tacit glossing of spines,

the ruffling of silk cravats,
readers mine and quarry into translations,

footnotes, seventeenth editions.
He brushes past, polite as hair tonic,

pausing, here and there, to ask the location of
The Anthology of Things He Wished He'd Said.

Chins lift slowly. Fingers wax
into furrowed brows, as French polishers might.

When directed to enquiries
he does not find the Librarian.

It is always just one second past twelve.
The best quips are long overdue.

In the Senior Common Room

A swarm without a hive has no master.
—Law of the Roman Republic

The Divinity master kept bees: his apiary set
beyond the Second Eleven's outfield,
at the gorse-hedged limit of the grounds.
Long, summer afternoons they watched him
going among hives through wedged shadows,
and those who couldn't hold a bat straight

opted 'off Games' to go to the honeybee
and learn how diligent she is.
The breaking of the comb-honey's wax capping
was what they came to cherish—
an Arcadian crème brûlée
they smeared on hot crumpets, spooned into tea

those autumn nights in the oak-panelled study.
He told them bees were blessed when leaving Eden,
became handmaids of the Most High;
how Bretons believed them the tears of Christ crucified;
how they sing 'Hosanna in Excelsis'
on the stroke of midnight each Christmas Eve,

for which he would bless them with slabs of fondant.
They wore the angry blotches on their knuckles
proudly; and, when a swarm of errant drones,
drunk on gorse flowers, flew a careless scrawl
through the lunch hall window,
to rummage among the treacle puddings,

and prompt HM—worn beyond patience
by years of bee-related complaint—
to pronounce, 'Since you cannot control them,
these pests are no more welcome here
than disease,' they replied, 'But
how do you know they're *our* bees?'

Bee’s Nocturne

Bee waxed midnight.
Moon silvered
over lawn and brick,

while Bee muttered
through cloudy cairns of sky,
between hellebore

and jasmine, clenching
his barbed sting tight,
like a sniper’s

rifle-trigger,
or the last, hard word
of the argument.

Exemplum

I hate to tell a cautionary tale, but
consider the fate of the Gnostic's ghost,

how sadly too late it hankered after a body,
coveted the thrill of silk shirt against skin,

dreamt of an itch it might scratch;
the pathos invoked by its transparent ardour

as it loitered by the massage parlour;
its plaintive sighs at stubbed toes, and sneezes.

How often it was found with its hand in the fire,
or rubbing its back on a stretch of barbed wire.

How nothing could dim its repentant desire,
not even the priest with bell, book

and candle, who explained
that for unreclaimed heretic and heathen

the afterlife is . . . whatever they'd imagined.
I know you'll come back. I leave the door open.

Waves

Waves are not frightening when they break:
their terror lies in brooding on the seabed.

~

He lay with her awhile on a hotel bed
as waves of light spent themselves upon them;

salt lick of coastal light breaking
from the imperceptible meeting point

of sky and sea—from distance, into harbour.
Occasional traffic might have been waves.

Heatwaves from concrete, beach-front buildings.
Jetsam of picnics and holiday lovers.

~

Only to wash up back on his accustomed street—
curtains and custom; a seeming mindfulness

in routine tasks; the two of them like
bipolar moons orbiting an atmosphere;

the tide stretched taut as the *O*
made between flexed bowstring and tensile bow;

the great wave that will break them
brooding, unspeakable—only so long.

He found solace in kicking through
dreck and bladderwrack.

~

He sleeps through the traffic.
A thin blanket waves over him.

The sky through bedsit windows
tilting on its axis, like see-saw horizons

through the windows of night-boats
sailing one way to Permanence.

Eleven Ante-Meridian

Amid snug lamps, cream cotton curtains,
familial upholstery, wearing nothing

but slippers and late morning,
many-angled sunlight, she reclines—

studies sycamore seeds spinning
carelessly down to the street.

A hard-won set of two-slatted, lathe-turned
dining chairs preserves her dignity.

She allows his absence to thicken,
like her best New England chowder;

collects from the mahogany dresser
the note he delivered to the mahogany dresser,

to read again of his catholic tastes,
their wilting passion—to measure loss

with words light as the husk
of a sycamore seed.

Accident

He shifts, moulding his frame
to the bath's curves, and soaks,

noting the hot tap's dripping,
its arrhythmic timpani:

a one; a one-two; then, a minim rest—
the time required to swell

another pear-shaped mass
of sufficient gravitas.

These occult and ineffable
frequencies of nature:

plane trees plucked by wind;
occasional windscreen glare;

her stepping from the kerb, just then;
the ebb and flow of luck he needs

not to have been noticed
as he drove from the scene.

'An accident,' he says aloud;
and, for a moment, it sounds okay;

so, he tries it again . . .
Maybe it's the echo off the tiles,

or the false theatricality
of unheard soliloquy—

the way words leak their meanings
when too much repeated?

This one's cracked.
Something swells slowly

to critical mass
on the other side of a word.

Self-Portrait in a Rear-View Mirror

The road home cuts through a floodplain
pocked with pylons, like those we climbed
when children, fleeing the suburb
in expedition to the river.

Myth warned of leeches
snicking piss-warm shallows;
of the kid who peeled wet trunks
to find one bristling on his bell-end;

of pike teeth snagging foreskins
like barbed wire. We waded in
timidly, until a silt ooze
between toes made us hazard

our bodies against currents.
A dense silage-musk seemed to bend
willow boughs low over cold water—
hopeful parabolas we dived

under skies too pure to conceive
drowning, too lucid to believe
the cautionary tales beloved
of adults. Distant tractor engines.

Lowing of milk-glutted cattle.
Marsh bird cackle. Sudden wing-flap
from green rushes. Barely one mile
from the industrial estate,

the motorway, the power plant
(though too far by half
we found in an emergency).
Now, the river is widening

as I drive into the city,
and the pylons retreat behind
my furrowed brow in the rear-view mirror:
the fresh-ploughed thoughts of the child.

Seven Stations of a Record Collection

After Paul Muldoon

Johnny Thunders and the Heartbreakers

L.A.M.F.

Johnny Thunders came to our house when I was four.
My brother, his roadie, in whimsical spirit,
dropped in with the band on an impromptu visit.
They were booked at Top Rank: their '77 tour.

They slouched on our sofas, fidgeting with their hair.
Mother poured them tea, offered biscuits, crossed her arms.
'More tea, Mr Thunders?' Her voice indifferent and spare,
but they all used the coasters, cupped crumbs in their palms.

At the same age she, too, defied convention—
or so I've since gleaned with some well-applied questions
when leafing through family photograph albums.
But *then*, she stayed silent. They all felt the tension,

scratched needle-pocked arms, yawned; then, were gone.
She soaked the teacups in bleach, and held me too long.

Rod Stewart
Atlantic Crossing

The soundtrack to family gatherings on Canvey,
while I played *Monopoly* on Nan's threadbare Wilton
with a friend I'd deny was imaginary
when he swapped Mayfair for Angel Islington.

Omnipresent, even on the Canvey Club's jukebox,
to which the family decamped once Nan had her gin.
My brother hustled darts for a Sunday joint, or Scotch;
some gold-toothed losel slipped my aunt a Mickey Finn.

Near closing, inexorable as income tax,
danced a clownish charade of Rod-a-likes,
pouting and laughing under blue-gel-screened lights:
paste-buckled grey slip-ons, white socks, *Farah* slacks;

bared chests and necklines with a tangerine tan
from the high street solarium: un-American.

NICK CAVE

From Her to Eternity

I knew her by reputation before we met:
expelled from Roedean, from the family mansion;
legend told she rode Godiva-style (for a bet)
down Lyndhurst High Street; barred from The Stag Inn

for being 'Mad as a bag of adders.'
So, I was prepared when she led through moonlit trees
to her Romany caravan, dealt 'The Lovers',
began to teach me female anatomy.

I couldn't reconcile her neatly-clipped vowels
with the cheap patchouli; snakebite-and-black
with Cancale oysters; the van with the Chelsea flat.
She left, one night. I don't know how she lives now,

and I wouldn't know where to pick up the scent.
I let the walls close in, year by year; but she went.

James Taylor
Mud Slide Slim and the Blue Horizon

always returns me to that converted London
bus—home of the veteran, red-bearded traveller—
where I couched with smugglers, swigging *Jameson*,
awaiting the return of their merchant ventures.

Each year they'd convert banknotes to contraband,
entrust one of their crew to sail the slow roads
from Fez in a barely roadworthy *Transit* van.
One night he was late. They shared suspicions in code.

Sweet baby James was crooning when we heard tyres.
The relief with which they clasped him in their arms
made that fear less real, the outlaw life more charmed.
Since then, it's true, I've pursued conventional desires;

but, when the record plays I'm seventeen again—
wishing the outlaws safe through hostile terrain.

BRUCE COCKBURN
In the Falling Dark

Exeter, then: fey folk fayres; garrets in Gandy
Street; hand-to-mouth homespuns; idiot idealism;
juvenilia; kickshaws; ley line lollardy;
municipal murals; neo-paganism

in patchouli-perfumed parks; quests for quondam quacks;
reliquaries; saturnalian scholastics
squabbling over Scotch; twopenny, street mission tracts;
unexpected *in vino veritas* hysterics;

wandering home wet along the banks of the Exe;
youth, yearning for a Zen-like zeitgeist; attic
attitudes; bourgeois bohemians; catholic
tastes; dithyrambic dirges they strove to perfect.

Two became lawyers, one a teacher, one a clerk.
That world faded out like an overheard remark.

David Briggs

Landscape and Liability

You were landscape, and I—the way I was—hiking
through that nettle-strewn wilderness and startled by
everything: a faint bleat; thurump of quickening
hooves. We climbed the summit to a mercurial sky.

Two hawks hung on the wind, fluttered like dust cloth
on antique furniture. Then, wave-like, they advanced,
trailing shadows that swept across the mountain trough
and lost their shape. You knew we hadn't a chance

of finding the primrose path from your mountain themes
to my lowland plot. Those spare, thread-needled lines
of farmland: lines drawn by sweat and unquiet minds;
lines by which we chart ourselves back from flawed schemes.

I finished recording, and you left, the same day.
I sold a few—mostly to friends. Gave the rest away.

David Sylvian

Damage

Two quick raps on the windscreen roused me. Hurled from
sleep, I saw myself in third person: haggard,
white male in parked car, comatose on the wheel arm,
engine running. From this point of view I, too, would

be inclined to ask myself if I was all right.
Three months separated; divorce papers to peruse;
full-time job; four-hundred mile round trip each fortnight
to see my daughter. I can barely tie my own shoes,

but I'm no suicide, just tired. Thank you for checking.
And you're right: it's not the end of the world, as such;
but I need to know: was it me? Her? By how much?
Endless appraisal, like an engine left idling,

going always nowhere, only belching fumes.
Damage on permanent loop in part-furnished rooms.

Seafaring

'... And yet he who aspires to the ocean always has the yearning.'
— *The Seafarer* translated by S.A.J. Bradley

Forked spears fretted earthward;
sky behemoths bellowed; rain-moats
forced footsteps: still they surged seaward,

as westerly breakers broke over
a beached boat, and stars punched
dents in night's metalwork.

Wearily, they waded through backwash
and heaved the hull heavenward.
Rocking in the rip and surge

their vessel swept them swiftly
over the stern and out to sea—
never to harbour, always to flee.

Winter Music

In the cold earth, the fat turf, ravens claw
fretboards of stubble and potato root.

Washboard hands, scrubbed raw in Arctic air,
keep time to the wingbeat of wasteland ravens.

This is all there is, save granite outcrops
black with mizzle and quarrying:

what will they make of the song thrush
when the hurdy-gurdy of January

churns out across sky? As wind cracks snow
from crags, tugs at loose roof-thatch,

the villagers sing vigil, from the rough-hewn
harbour of heresy, for those still at sea.

Snow

Contrary to popular belief, the Inuit do not have more words for snow than do speakers of English . . . Counting generously, experts can come up with about a dozen.

— Stephen Pinker *The Language Instinct*

Say there are no words for lawyer
in the Inuit tongue; yet, perhaps,
a dozen by which to adjudicate

snowfall. Say there is no English word
for the particular spectacle
of aurora-lit snowfall,

while for lawyer we have: barrister,
attorney, brief, solicitor, silk,
advocate, justice, litigator,

magistrate, counsel, prosecutor,
perhaps even jurisprudentia.
And it follows that in the land

where they speak only statistics
there will be a sworn affidavit
against each irregular snowflake.

But you are advised not to impugn
the government of such climes
for burying truth beneath an icy

deluge of little, whitely-lying words.
Some thoughts will simply fail to settle
in our language, or gather only

in obscure, mountainous regions.
This thought itself may fail to find
the climate necessary to its

survival and, so, melt gently
on the thick muscle of my tongue
as might *tla* (snow), *tlaslo* (slow falling snow),

or *penstla* (merely the idea of snow).

Cultural Static

The manufacturers of cultural viruses
were hawking liquid pep-me-ups
laced with pharmaceutical cocaine,

pimping rolls in the hay with the Dow(ager) Jones—
long withering out young men's revenue
all along the Hammersmith Flyover.

Economically lubricious, perhaps?
But it played merry hell with my concentration,
like viral pop-ups interrupting my research

on the lesser-known sobriquets
for eighteenth-century bordellos.
It was no better in the eldritch capital—

gallery attendants neglecting the finer etiquettes,
crashing into our impromptu game of
'Join the Black Dots in *Marriage à la mode*'.

But the reviews augured well for Doctor Faustus
in conversation with Doctor Octopus,
on the Four Stages of Cruelty, at the Hunterian.

And we'd good seats: centre aisle, middle-row stalls.
No creaking backrests. It wasn't that the argument
was difficult to follow; more a consequence

of the ill-timed fanfare of a meta-ironic,
polyphonic ringtone which, these days,
I suppose, is what passes for personality.

Conjugation in C Minor

She was a 'cello. He was the invention
of radio. She swooned; became a swallow,

with feathers of white, black and aquamarine.
He foresaw glory in distant war.

Briefly, they became Pachelbel's Canon:
she reminded him of formal gardens.

He fell wounded in battle.
The military psychiatrist discerned

he was a lark, but he sang out of tune.
He escaped in his shirt: unbuttoned;

unironed; they became Sandinistas,
bribed the electorate with cigars

and avocados. They became folk songs
in every mouth of the Republic.

She evolved into Vesuvius
erupting over Pompeii, flooding the Forum

with lava. Thousands died, were fossilised.
Those that escaped worked together

at the foot of her slopes, knowing flood,
fire or earthquake could claim them anywhere.

Sagely, they planted till cities grew.
She became gin; he, the pressure valve

of a steam engine. It was raining.
Twins were conceived, rurally.

That night, she was a juniper; he was pistons,
turbines and industrial revolution.

Their progeny inherited these sorrows.
They sing them as ballads from market-barrows.

The Woodlander

It’s said he produced a hand-plucked pheasant
on the tines of a toasting fork, stuffed with morels;
cooked it on the coal-effect hearth, so nonchalant,
as though bivouacking among the faux oak panels,

canned music, and enamelled real ale ads—
till fat-spit and mirth awakened the ire
of the barman with bugger-grips (surly-to-mad
at the best of times), who made straight for the fire

and barred Our Fred without hope of parole.
Since the refurbishment it’s not for me—
piss-weak lager, and olives, served on a doily.
If ever I run my own pub, I swear on the Dole

there’ll be fiddles and moonshine till sunup Doomsday,
and Fred at the barbecue. I’ll do it my way.

The Philosophical Bowling Shoe Counter Attendant

The world has nothing to show more fair

than a bowling ball careering down reinforced parquet,
as though possessed by perpetual motion,

to scatter tenpins like cannon-fodder.
Thirty-five last week. Still forced to suffer
your demands for red-white, co-respondent

shoes across my polymer-blue, fag-burnt
counter; but, do not doubt the palpable
fear at each regional bowling final
when I take the alley. Lock-up duty

is sublime: Wagner over the tannoy,

as I perfect the side-spinning curve-ball
till dawn. Then, a philosophical

shit, shave and shower in the gents;
whore's breakfast of coffee and cigarette,
to disguise my presence as unofficial tenant.

Say what you will of ambition;
have you resolved the duality
of the day job and the dream—the Jungian
thing, the arc between aim and accuracy?

My Year of Culture

After Kathleen Ossip

We're walking home late from the theatre,
my lover and I. She's wearing pearls
and a linen trouser suit—it was a 'well-made' play.
'Sweetheart,' I say,
'the writer drank snake blood for inspiration.'
She flicks her tongue.

We're lying in bed reading the supplements,
my lover and I. I'm wearing yellow socks;
the D.A.B. can't find a signal—she hopes I kept the receipt.
'Ma Cherie,' I joke,
'the static between stations is an echo from the Big Bang.'
She grapples the bedclothes.

We're in the Blake room at Tate Britain,
my lover and I. She's using her catalogue
as a fan—it's the hottest May since records began.
'Hey,' she taunts,
'there's nothing shameful in going naked.'
I loosen my tie.

We're drinking gin and tonic near the Opera House,
my lover and I. I'm wearing a russet, silk suit
with matching Turk's head cufflinks—we've seen *Otello*.
'Sweetheart,' I ask,
'would you take a pill that healed existential doubt?'
She whistles through her teeth.

We're in a gondola on the Grand Canal,
my lover and I. She's wearing white jeans
and *Ray-Bans*—we arrived by train from Milan.
'Hey,' the gondolier says,
'you want I show you the house of Lord Byron?'
We shrug. We've seen it before.

We're in the front row at a reading
by the next great Oulipo stylist,
my lover and I. She's wearing yellow culottes
and orange *Converse All-Stars*—everyone here's a writer.
'Hey,' she whispers,
'what's the optimum lexical density of a reading?'
The poet delivers a poem made of snarls.

Reflection

Each morning, squat on the cuckstool,
scranning the *LRB*

(a liberal and informed member of the citizenry),
thin-socked, two-score, wistful,

he ponders his bran-free regularity;
and, sometimes, washing his hands

in the new *Heritage* suite,
surprised by his reflection's seeming perspicacity,

something akin to self-knowledge
slithers between his fingers

beneath the running tap;
a few, fat dabs of buttery sunlight

spotting the mirror's illusory depth
of that more promising Otherwhere:

as though he might leave himself behind
and walk out, a dash lighter,

into a new, more exciting, hallway.

Bloomsday

'Now who is that lankylooking galoot over there in the macintosh? Now who is he I'd like to know? Now, I'd give a trifle to know who he is.'

—JAMES JOYCE *Ulysses*

I wake myself laughing: an absurd word adrift
on the tide of a dream, in a cork-stoppered bottle,
obscure on the shore as Crusoe's odd footprint.
The kitchen's a comfort: cupboards and *Kilner* jars,
milk in a carton and mail on the table.
Yet, even these unfocused, childhood photographs,
salvaged like jetsam from a family reunion,
seem brittle as ropes frayed in the brine.
Raised for inspection, as a porcelain cup
between finger and thumb,
the idea of the Self seems fragile, an artifice.
And Memory's only a clock-stopped room,
through which I'm taking a dust-fingered stroll,
finding the furniture differently organised.
Unable to recall the exact disposition
of a sideboard, a lamp, those decorative fire irons,
I scan these self-righteous critiques of my life,
penned and delivered by the indignant ghost
of my sixteen-year-old self.
He leers at my shoulder as I slit each envelope
with the stainless steel blade
of my pearl-handled letter opener;
watches me read, mouthing his phrases—
all cod-philosophy and plagiarised lyrics.
The effort required to think at his pitch
is a self-conscious thing, like dialling the number
of a friend you've lost touch with,
of an aunt who might disclose family secrets.
When first I was blown by the storm
to this city, this street I now live in
would have frowned from its windows

like an interview panel; yet, now, its plane trees
and Edwardian lampposts are courteous yeomen
as I take the corner and thumb-flick my ciggie.
The 'bus pulls in. A rampant pack
of feral children in tracksuits and wife-beaters
mopes in the aisle next to the luggage rack.
One appropriates a red umbrella
to wear in his thighs as a tumescent phallus,
with which he begins to solicit indecently
first his chums, then the rest of us,
hunkered behind paperbacks and communal *Metros*,
fearing his veto of unwritten etiquette.
Centuries pass as we dawdle in traffic
and they shout obscenities at passing pedestrians.
I take my own stop; think how agreeable
the City would be if everyone spoke
with the same clipped precision
and ear for the epigram or scathing *bon mot*
as the characters in *The Draughtsman's Contract*;
and filter the 'bus scene through this fond whimsy:
the kid with the brolly mocks a latterday Pooter:

> *That scowl of bourgeois disapproval*
> *is as black as the cloth of your pinstripe trews;*
> *yet, my good sir, if you'll permit me to comment*
> *there's nothing of substance in one or the other.*

Ah! for a world of Johnsonian wit.
Before I know it I'm halfway along
the gentrified harbour, where apartments go up
like *Meccano* constructions.
But the park's still here, I'm relieved to discover.
There's a time I freewheeled these avenues,
thinking the ideal narrative pace
was the equivalent of a bicycle ride;
my daughter, then, still hitting her milestones;
before the prognosis, the breakdown, divorce,

the tactfully-synchronised bedside vigils
in increasingly-specialised children's hospitals.
How many years? A decade,
yet only a district, away. And look now:
tousled scallywags named Mungo and Oscar
launch febrile kites on a mischievous breeze;
picnicking clans play a few rowdy innings
of hit-and-run cricket;
a 'Save Our Allotments' fundraising fête,
with unsigned, indigenous, jazz-folk collectives,
packing crates stuffed with mud-flecked broccoli,
and garage-sale stall holders
in Paisley headscarves and Peruvian knitwear;
acrid perfume of jazz-folk woodbine
from the fair-weather student
sprawled on the grass bank as on a *chaise longue*,
a translation of Proust
raised in one hand as an Edwardian parasol.
When Memory is a public park
filled with familiar, yet strangely dressed, ghosts,
through which we take a hopeful saunter . . .
best not to rummage among the flowerbeds.
    I take the corner—
    raised for inspection,
    between finger and thumb,
    the idea of the Self—
    I thumb-flick my ciggie,
    and wake myself laughing.

Pulse

This language in which we write ourselves
upon each other, untranslatable

from bed-sheet pages: muscular verbs,
two lines conjoined by feminine rhyme,

without narrative; lyrical sonnet to sex
in a continuous present, running firm

and slow across line breaks, bending
like blossomed boughs in a sun-flecked

orchard, clear river laughing, surprise ice
drifting: we're a pulse in the veins

of Arcadian satyrs, about to be uttered,
about to be sounded, with the same ground

for meaning as any song, word or book
when oblivion beckons blissfully.